D1646229

Quick and Easy
Midweek Meals

Wendy Sweetser

Contents

Published exclusively for J Sainsbury plc
Stamford House Stamford Street
London SE1 9LL

by Martin Books
Simon & Schuster Consumer Group
Grafton House 64 Maids Causeway
Cambridge CB5 8DD

First published November 1994

ISBN 0 85941 872 3

Printed and bound in the UK by Bath Press Colourbooks
Design: Green Moore Lowenhoff
Photography: Clive Streeter
Styling: Maria Kelly
Food preparation: Kathy Man
Typesetting: Goodfellow & Egan Ltd, Cambridge

Pictured on the front cover: Chicken with Rainbow Peppers
(page 32)

Introduction

When you've had a busy day at work, the last thing you want is to spend hours in the kitchen preparing the evening meal, especially if you know the family will be home at any moment, starving-hungry and demanding their dinners. It's not always easy, though, to come up with ideas for quick, easy suppers that are good to eat and don't rely heavily on convenience or ready-prepared foods. However, by carefully mixing store-cupboard items with fresh ingredients, it is possible to make many delicious and appetising dishes in the shortest possible time.

In this book, all the dishes can be prepared and cooked in half an hour, as long as you organise yourself to prepare one ingredient while another is cooking. Some of us work much faster in the kitchen than others, so if you find that a recipe takes a bit longer than it should do, once you know your way around it you ought to be much quicker next time.

The recipes in the book concentrate on small cuts of meat, fish and other ingredients that can be cooked quickly and have little waste, as it's obviously not possible to roast a joint or cook a casserole in half an hour. You need to switch the oven on for very few of the dishes: the majority of them are cooked on the hob or under the grill.

Some of the meat recipes will benefit from longer marinating times, so if you can, prepare the dish ready for cooking the night before and, when you get in from work, your preparation is done and the food just needs to be cooked.

Except where indicated, all the recipes in the book will serve four people but quantities can be halved or doubled without any problems in most instances.

Some recipes in this book contain lightly cooked eggs. Consumers are reminded of the advice from the Department of Health that it would be prudent for consumers, particularly those most vulnerable, such as pregnant women, babies and young children, elderly people and invalids, to avoid eating raw or lightly cooked eggs or dishes made from them. Readers are therefore advised to use their own judgement when selecting recipes.

The majority of the dishes are designed for family suppers, but if you've got midweek guests for dinner, some, like Trout with Mushroom, Tomato and Fennel Sauce (page 28), Chicken with Rainbow Peppers (page 32) or Pork with Honey and Mustard Sauce (page 36) could easily be upgraded to main courses suitable for entertaining. Just add a colourful salad, some crusty bread and cheese and a bottle of wine and you'll have a dinner party to be proud of.

STORECUPBOARD SUGGESTIONS

The following is a list of the storecupboard items used in the recipes in this book. If you are making a recipe and find you don't have all the items listed, it's often possible to substitute something you do have for the missing one. For example, in Balti Chicken (page 34), if you don't have all the spices listed, you can use curry powder or paste instead. Similarly different pastas can be used to those specified, for example, spaghetti instead of tagliatelle, or fusilli instead of penne, and ingredients such as nuts, oil, canned pulses, sugar, vinegar, mustard and canned fish, can be varied according to what you have available.

Almond essence

Bottled sauces: brown, cranberry, creamed horseradish, hoisin, oyster, red pesto, soy (dark and light), Tabasco, tomato pasta sauce or passata (sieved tomatoes)

Canned bolognese sauce

Canned fish: anchovies, salmon, sardines, tuna

Canned fruit: pineapple pieces, pineapple slices in fruit juice.

Canned pulses: beans in tomato sauce, butter beans, cannellini beans, chick-peas, flageolet beans, red kidney beans

Canned soup: condensed cream of celery, condensed cream of mushroom

Canned tomatoes: chopped, chopped with herbs, plum

Canned vegetables: new potatoes, sweetcorn, sweetcorn with peppers

Creamed coconut

Crisps

Dried pasta: farfalle, fusilli, penne, quick-cook macaroni, tagliatelle

Dry breadcrumbs

Flour: cornflour, plain, strong plain

Grated parmesan cheese

Mayonnaise

Meringue shells

Mustard: coarse-grain, Dijon, dry mustard

Nuts: chopped mixed nuts, ground almonds, walnuts

Oats: medium oatmeal, porridge oats

Oil: groundnut, olive, sesame, sunflower, vegetable

Packet cheese sauce

Preserves: honey, seedless raspberry jam, smooth peanut butter, strawberry jam

Ready-to-eat dried apricots

Rice: boil-in-the-bag basmati, canned long-grain, easy-cook long-grain and wild, saffron savoury rice

Spices: black pepper, chilli powder, cinnamon, coriander, cumin, curry powder or paste, ginger, salt, sesame seeds, turmeric

Stock cubes: beef, chicken, fish, pork, vegetable

Sugar: caster or granulated, demarara, icing, light brown

Sun-dried tomatoes

Sweet sherry

Tomato purée

Wine vinegar: red, white

RECIPE NOTES

All recipes in this book give ingredients in both metric (g, ml, etc.) and Imperial (oz, pints, etc.) measures. Use either set of quantities, but not a mixture of both, in any one recipe.

All teaspoons and tablespoons are level, unless otherwise stated.

1 teaspoon = a 5 ml spoon;

1 tablespoon = a 15 ml spoon.

Egg size is medium (size 3), unless otherwise stated.

Vegetables and fruit are medium-size unless otherwise stated.

Freshly ground black pepper should be used throughout.

PREPARATION AND COOKING TIMES

Preparation and cooking times are included at the head of the recipes as a general guide; preparation times, especially, are approximate and timings are usually rounded to the nearest 5 minutes.

Preparation times include the time taken to prepare ingredients in the list.

The cooking times given at the heads of the recipes denote cooking periods when the dish can be left largely unattended, e.g. baking, and not the total amount of cooking for the recipe. Always read and follow the timings given for the steps of the recipe in the method.

Egg and Cheese Dishes

When you want a meal in a hurry, eggs and cheese fit the bill every time, providing a variety of wholesome, appetising dishes. Turn eggs into Spanish- or Italian-style flat omelettes packed with your favourite ingredients; hard-boil them and add to a crisp vegetable salad; or scramble with bacon and mushrooms and spoon over muffins or toast. And, with so many different cheeses available now, you could probably cook a cheesy dish every day for months and never eat the same one twice! From full-flavoured Cheddar to mild mozzarella or tangy blue Stilton, there's something to suit every taste.

Bacon and Mushroom Scramble

Preparation and cooking time: 20 minutes.
Freezing: not recommended. Serves 4.

A new supper version of an old breakfast favourite. Cook the bacon until lightly browned, and the vegetables until tender, before adding the eggs.

4 muffins, split

8 eggs

2 tablespoons single cream or milk

1 tablespoon vegetable or sunflower oil

75 g (3 oz) bacon, chopped

1 small leek, sliced

50 g (2 oz) baby button mushrooms, halved or
    left whole

salt and pepper

snipped fresh chives, to garnish

❶ Lightly toast the cut sides of the muffins. Keep them warm in a low oven.

❷ Beat the eggs with the cream or milk and seasoning.

❸ Heat the oil in a large saucepan and fry the bacon pieces for 2 minutes, stirring frequently.

❹ Add the leek and the mushrooms and fry for a further 5 minutes, until the bacon pieces are lightly browned and the leek and mushrooms are soft.

❺ Pour in the egg mixture and cook over a low heat, stirring frequently, until the eggs are just set.

❻ Spoon the egg mixture over the toasted muffins and serve sprinkled with snipped chives.

Cheddar Aigrettes with Tomato Sauce

Preparation and cooking time: 30 minutes.
Freezing: not recommended. Serves 4.

Crisp, savoury puffs of deep-fried choux pastry make an unusual supper dish. Accompany them with a mildly spiced tomato sauce and serve on their own or with grilled bacon, sausages or beef burgers.

For the aigrettes:
100 g (3½ oz) strong plain flour
¼ teaspoon dry mustard
150 ml (¼ pint) water
50 g (2 oz) butter, cut into small pieces
2 eggs, beaten
50 g (2 oz) mature Cheddar cheese, grated
oil for deep-frying

2 tablespoons grated parmesan cheese, plus
    extra to garnish (optional)
salt and pepper
For the tomato sauce:
300 ml (½ pint) napoletana or other tomato
    pasta sauce
1 tablespoon chopped fresh marjoram
a few drops of Tabasco sauce

❶ To make the aigrettes, sieve the flour and mustard together over a sheet of greaseproof paper.

❷ Heat the water and butter in a saucepan until the butter melts. Bring to a fast boil, remove from the heat and tip in all the flour.

❸ Beat with a wooden spoon until the mixture is smooth and leaves the sides of the pan. Cool for a few minutes. Beat in the eggs a little at a time, adding the cheese and seasoning with the last addition of egg.

❹ Heat the oil in a large saucepan or deep-fat fryer to 170°C/325°F or until a small cube of bread browns in the oil in 1 minute. Drop teaspoonfuls of the mixture into the hot oil and fry in batches for 4 to 5 minutes until puffed and golden brown.

❺ Drain the aigrettes on kitchen paper, sprinkle them with the 2 tablespoons of parmesan cheese and keep them warm in a low oven.

❻ To make the sauce, heat the tomato sauce in a pan until bubbling gently. Stir in the marjoram and Tabasco.

❼ Serve the aigrettes with the sauce, sprinkled with a little more grated parmesan cheese, if you like.

Cheesy Farfalle with Leeks and Frankfurters

Preparation and cooking time: 25 minutes.
Freezing: recommended, without the fried bread. Serves 4.

Use a packet cheese sauce for this recipe, or two 300 g cartons of four-cheese pasta sauce from the chiller cabinet.

50 g (2 oz) butter

500 g (1 lb) leeks, cut into 1 cm (½-inch) slices

250 g (8 oz) farfalle (pasta bows)

600 ml (1 pint) cheese sauce

8 frankfurters, cut into 2.5 cm (1-inch) lengths

75 g (3 oz) Cheddar cheese, grated

2 tablespoons dry breadcrumbs

oil for frying

4 slices of bread, crusts removed

salt and pepper

❶ Heat the butter in a large saucepan and add the leeks. Cover and cook over a gentle heat for about 10 minutes, or until the leeks are tender.

❷ While the leeks are frying, cook the farfalle according to the packet instructions. Drain.

❸ Preheat the grill to hot.

❹ Add the cheese sauce to the leeks, bring to the boil and stir in the farfalle, frankfurters and seasoning.

❺ Spoon into a shallow heatproof dish and sprinkle over the grated Cheddar and the breadcrumbs.

❻ Grill until the top is golden. Meanwhile, cut each slice of bread into four triangles. Heat a little oil in a frying-pan and the bread fry until golden brown. Accompany the cheesy farfalle with the fried bread.

Chorizo Tortilla

Preparation and cooking time: 25 minutes.
Freezing: not recommended. Serves 4.

This traditional Spanish omelette is excellent eaten hot or cold. Chorizos are small, spicy sausages sold alongside other packaged cold meats. You could use salami, frankfurters or chopped ham instead, if you prefer. Serve with a tomato, spring onion and basil salad.

500 g (1 lb) potatoes, peeled and cut into small chunks

2 tablespoons olive or sunflower oil

3 chorizos, cut into 1 cm (½-inch) slices

6 large eggs (size 1–2)

salt and pepper

2 tablespoons snipped fresh chives, to garnish

❶ Cook the potatoes in lightly salted boiling water until just tender. Drain.

❷ Heat the oil in a large frying-pan, about 25 cm (10 inches) in diameter. Add the potatoes and fry over a medium heat until lightly browned.

❸ Add the chorizos and cook for 2 minutes.

❹ Beat the eggs with the seasoning and pour them into the pan. Cook until the eggs have set on the bottom but are still runny on top. Meanwhile, preheat the grill to hot.

❺ Slide the pan under the grill and cook until the eggs have set on top.

❻ Garnish with the chives and serve at once.

Ciabatta Bruschetta

Preparation and cooking time: 20 minutes.
Freezing: recommended (reheat from frozen). Serves 2–4.

Italian ciabatta bread can be turned into a crisp, pizza-style snack by adding lots of colourful, tasty toppings. Vary the toppings according to your own personal preference and what you have available. On its own, the loaf will serve two; if accompanied with a green salad it should serve four, as long as you add plenty of topping.

1 ciabatta loaf, split lengthways

3 tablespoons olive oil

6 tablespoons tomato pasta sauce

150 g (5 oz) mozzarella cheese, sliced

125 g (4 oz) sliced salami or Parma ham

4 anchovy fillets

¼ green pepper, de-seeded and sliced thinly

4 mushrooms, sliced thinly

1 shallot or small onion, sliced thinly

pepper

❶ Preheat the oven to Gas Mark 5/190°C/375°F.

❷ Place the two halves of the ciabatta on a baking sheet (crust down) and brush the cut sides with 2 tablespoons of the olive oil.

❸ Spread the ciabatta with the pasta sauce and top with the cheese slices, salami or Parma ham, anchovy fillets, green pepper, mushrooms and shallot or onion. Season with black pepper.

❹ Brush the green pepper, mushroom and shallot or onion slices with the remaining oil and bake in the oven for 10 minutes, or until the bruschetta is hot and the cheese is bubbling. Serve at once.

Mozzarella, Roasted Pepper and Avocado Salad

Preparation time: 20 minutes. Freezing: not recommended. Serves 4.

Roasting peppers gives them a deliciously sweet flavour and makes them more digestible. Serve with warm focaccia bread.

1 each red, green and yellow peppers
300 g (10 oz) mozzarella cheese
2 small avocados, sliced thinly
For the dressing:
4 tablespoons extra-virgin olive oil

1 tablespoon lime or lemon juice
1 tablespoon chopped fresh chervil
salt and pepper
a few small basil or chervil leaves, to garnish

❶ Grill the peppers all over until their skins are charred and blackened, turning regularly. Place the peppers in a polythene bag, seal and leave until cool enough to handle.

❷ Peel the skins from the peppers. Cut the peppers into quarters and discard the core and seeds.

❸ Drain the mozzarella cheeses and cut them into thin slices.

❹ Arrange the peppers, cheese and avocado slices on serving plates.

❺ To make the dressing, mix together the oil, lime or lemon juice, chervil and seasoning. Spoon over the salad and garnish with a few small basil or chervil leaves.

Ravioli with Blue Cheese and Broccoli Sauce

Preparation and cooking time: 15 minutes.
Freezing: not recommended. Serves 4.

Look for packs of fresh ravioli with a meat or vegetable filling (either would be suitable for this recipe) in the chiller cabinet with other fresh pastas and sauces.

250 g (8 oz) small broccoli florets
500 g (1 lb) fresh ravioli
125 g (4 oz) blue Stilton cheese, crumbled
50 g (2 oz) Edam cheese, grated

200 ml (7 fl oz) carton of crème fraîche
125 ml (4 fl oz) milk
1 tablespoon chopped fresh thyme
salt and pepper

❶ Cook the broccoli in lightly salted boiling water until just tender. Drain.

❷ Cook the ravioli according to the packet instructions. Drain.

❸ While the pasta is cooking, put the Stilton, Edam, crème fraîche and milk in a pan and heat gently until the cheeses have melted, stirring occasionally. Bring to simmering point.

❹ Remove the sauce from the heat and stir in the broccoli and thyme. Spoon the sauce over the cooked ravioli and season with salt and pepper. Serve at once.

Fish Dishes

Fish cooks quickly, has little waste and is good for you, too – so if you've never expanded your repertoire beyond fish and chips, now's the time to try! Cod and Corn Chowder (page 24), served with lots of crusty bread, will fill your family up when the weather's cold, and in summer no child will be able to resist a Sardine Burger (page 22), while you enjoy your Prawn Salad Niçoise (below), served outside. A wide range of fresh fish is available all year round, from traditional everyday favourites like cod and plaice, to newer varieties such as hoki – plus there's trout, shellfish and salmon when you're cooking to impress.

Prawn Salad Niçoise with Mozzarella Toasts

Preparation and cooking time: 20 minutes.
Freezing: not recommended. Serves 4.

A filling salad that makes an excellent supper dish when served with the cheesy toasts.

250 g (8 oz) cauliflower florets, divided in small pieces
12 cherry tomatoes, halved
1 green pepper, de-seeded and cut into small pieces
5 cm (2-inch) piece of cucumber, diced
a bag of mixed salad leaves, including radicchio and frisée
8 black olives
375 g (12 oz) prawns

For the dressing:
6 tablespoons virgin olive oil
2 tablespoons red wine vinegar
1 garlic clove, crushed
1 tablespoon chopped fresh tarragon
salt and pepper

For the mozzarella toasts:
1 french stick, cut in half lengthways
150 g (5 oz) mozzarella cheese, grated

❶ Cook the cauliflower in lightly salted boiling water until just tender. Drain and cool under cold water.

❷ Place the cauliflower in a large bowl and add the cherry tomatoes, green pepper, cucumber, salad leaves, olives and prawns.

❸ To make the dressing, whisk all the ingredients together and pour over the salad. Toss gently.

❹ To make the mozzarella toasts, preheat the grill and cut each half of the french stick in two or three. Toast the pieces of bread lightly on both sides. Sprinkle the mozzarella over the cut sides and grill until the cheese melts. Serve with the salad.

Salmon and Potato Gratin

Preparation and cooking time: 25 minutes.
Freezing: recommended. Serves 4.

Use a packet cheese sauce mix for this recipe or look for the cartons of fresh cheese sauce for pasta in the chiller cabinet. Serve with a crisp green salad.

25 g (1 oz) butter

125 g (4 oz) open-cup mushrooms, sliced

250 g (8 oz) broad beans, thawed if frozen

539 g can of new potatoes, drained and
    halved or quartered

600 ml (1 pint) cheese sauce

418 g can of red or pink salmon, drained

1 tablespoon snipped fresh chives

a small packet of plain crisps, crushed

50 g (2 oz) Cheddar or red Leicester cheese,
    grated

salt and pepper

❶ Melt the butter in a large saucepan and fry the mushrooms until soft.

❷ Stir in the broad beans, potatoes and cheese sauce, and heat gently until simmering.

❸ Remove the bones from the salmon and flake the flesh into the sauce mixture, with the chives. Simmer for 1 minute. Season to taste.

❹ Preheat the grill. Spoon the mixture into a shallow heatproof dish and sprinkle over the crushed crisps and grated cheese.

❺ Place the dish under the grill until the cheese melts and bubbles.

❻ Serve at once.

Sardine Burgers

Preparation and cooking time: 15 minutes.
Freezing: not recommended. Serves 4.

Serve the burgers with your favourite relishes, such as dill pickles, tomato chutney or corn relish. Accompany with oven chips or salad and coleslaw.

4 hamburger buns

2 tablespoons creamed horseradish or tartar
    sauce

5 cm (2-inch) piece of cucumber, sliced

2 tomatoes, sliced

4 lettuce leaves

2 × 120 g can of sardines in oil, drained

4 slices of Edam cheese

❶ Preheat the grill. Split the buns in half and lightly toast the cut sides. Leave the grill on.

❷ Spread the bottom half of each bun with the horseradish or tartar sauce.

❸ Divide the cucumber, tomato slices and the lettuce leaves between the buns, arrange the sardines on top and cover with the cheese slices.

❹ Return to the grill for 30 seconds or until the cheese begins to melt. Replace the lids of the buns and serve at once.

Cod in a Walnut and Oatmeal Crust

Preparation and cooking time: 25 minutes.
Freezing: recommended, after step 3. Serves 4.

Oatmeal and walnuts make a light, crisp coating for fish. Serve the cod with a tomato salad or grilled tomatoes.

3 tablespoons seasoned plain flour
¼ teaspoon dry mustard
4 × 175 g (6 oz) cod fillet, skinned
1 large egg (size 2), beaten
50 g (2 oz) porridge oats

25 g (1 oz) walnuts, chopped finely
oil for shallow-frying
orange wedges and watercress sprigs, to
   garnish

❶ Mix together the flour and mustard.
❷ Coat the cod fillets in the flour mixture and brush them with the beaten egg.
❸ Mix together the oats and walnuts and coat the fish with the mixture, pressing it firmly into the fillets.

❹ Heat some oil in a frying-pan and shallow-fry the fish in hot oil for about 5 minutes on each side until golden brown.
❺ Drain the fish on kitchen paper and serve garnished with orange wedges and watercress sprigs.

Cod and Corn Chowder

Preparation and cooking time: 25 minutes.
Freezing: recommended. Serves 4.

Serve this filling main-course soup with fried or toasted slices of crusty french bread.

50 g (2 oz) butter
8 spring onions, sliced
125 g (4 oz) button mushrooms, halved
1 courgette, sliced
50 g (2 oz) plain white flour
450 ml (¾ pint) milk
450 ml (¾ pint) fish stock

2 tablespoons tomato purée
1 tablespoon lemon juice
198 g can of sweetcorn with peppers, drained
375 g (12 oz) cod fillet, skinned and cut into
   small pieces
salt and pepper

❶ Melt the butter in a large saucepan and cook the spring onions, mushrooms and courgette for 3 minutes, stirring frequently.
❷ While the vegetables are cooking, stir the flour into a little of the milk until smooth. Add to the pan with the rest of the milk, stock, tomato purée and lemon juice.

❸ Bring to the boil, and cook, stirring, until thickened and smooth. Stir in the sweetcorn, cod and seasoning.
❹ Simmer for about 5 minutes or until the fish is cooked. Serve at once.

Creamy Smoked Haddock with Bacon and Cheese

Preparation and cooking time: 30 minutes.
Freezing: not recommended. Serves 4.

A tasty fish dish for smoked-haddock lovers. Serve with boiled or mashed potatoes and peas.

4 unsmoked streaky bacon rashers

500 g (1 lb) smoked haddock fillet, skinned and cut into chunks

142 ml (5 fl oz) carton of double cream

4 tomatoes, sliced

50 g (2 oz) Gruyère or Cheddar cheese, sliced

pepper

1 tablespoon chopped fresh parsley, to garnish

❶ Preheat the oven to Gas Mark 4/180°C/350°F.

❷ Grill or fry the bacon and cut each rasher into 3 pieces.

❸ Lay the smoked haddock in a shallow ovenproof dish and pour over the cream.

Top with the tomato slices and the bacon.

❹ Arrange the cheese slices over the top and season with ground black pepper.

❺ Cook, uncovered, in the oven until the fish flakes easily, about 10–15 minutes.

❻ Serve sprinkled with chopped parsley.

Mackerel and Tuna Pâté with Salad

Preparation time: 15 minutes. Freezing: not recommended. Serves 4.

This pâté should have a fairly coarse texture, so don't flake the fish too finely. Serve with crusty bread.

1 smoked mackerel fillet, skinned

185 g can of tuna in brine or oil, drained

125 g (4 oz) small prawns

grated zest and juice of ½ lemon

227 g (8 oz) carton of cottage cheese

3 tablespoons mayonnaise

pepper

For the salad:

2 Little Gem lettuces

2 celery sticks, sliced

4 tomatoes, quartered

1 avocado, chopped

❶ Flake the mackerel and tuna coarsely into a bowl. Stir in the prawns.

❷ Mix together the grated lemon zest and juice, cottage cheese, mayonnaise and pepper. Stir the mixture into the fish.

❸ To make the salad, divide the lettuces into individual leaves and arrange them on serving plates. Top with the celery slices, tomato quarters and chopped avocado.

❹ Pile the fish pâté on to the plate and chill until ready to serve.

Tuna with Green Beans

Preparation and cooking time: 15 minutes.
Freezing: not recommended. Serves 4.

Serve this salad with hot garlic bread.

250 g (8 oz) green beans, cut into 5 cm
   (2-inch) lengths
2 × 185 g can of tuna in oil
2 × 400 g can of flageolet beans, drained and
   rinsed
1 red pepper, de-seeded and sliced very thinly

For the dressing:
4 tablespoons virgin olive oil
2 tablespoons white wine vinegar
1 garlic clove, crushed
2 tablespoons chopped fresh parsley
salt and pepper

❶ Cook the beans in lightly salted boiling water for 3 minutes. Drain and cool under cold water. Place in a large bowl.

❷ Drain the tuna, reserving 2 tablespoons of the oil. Flake the tuna into large chunks and add to the green beans, with the flageolet beans and red pepper.

❸ To make the dressing, whisk together the reserved oil from the tuna, the olive oil, vinegar, garlic, parsley and seasoning.

❹ Pour the dressing over the salad and toss gently.

Trout with Mushroom, Tomato and Fennel Sauce

Preparation and cooking time: 30 minutes.
Freezing: not recommended. Serves 4.

Cooking fish in a foil parcel prevents it from drying out. Take the parcels to the table for diners to unwrap themselves. Serve with new potatoes and a green salad.

50 g (2 oz) button mushrooms, sliced
1 fennel bulb, chopped finely
400 g can of chopped tomatoes
1 tablespoon lemon juice

4 rainbow trout, cleaned
2 tablespoons olive oil
salt and pepper

❶ Preheat the oven to Gas Mark 4/180°C/350°F.

❷ Blanch the mushrooms and fennel in boiling water for 3 minutes. Drain and mix with the chopped tomatoes and lemon juice.

❸ Cut four sheets of foil, each one large enough to enclose a trout. Brush the sheets with the oil and place a fish in the centre of each.

❹ Spoon some of the tomato mixture into the cavity of each trout and the rest alongside. Season with salt and pepper. Seal the edges of the foil parcels tightly and place in a roasting tin.

❺ Cook in the oven for 15 to 20 minutes, or until the trout flesh flakes easily.

Meat and Poultry Dishes

Quick meals needn't mean giving up meat, if you choose small, lean cuts that need little cooking. Toss chicken pieces in spices and coconut for a delicious balti-style curry served with naan bread and pickles, stir-fry sesame-coated lamb in a sweet and sour sauce with colourful fresh vegetables or dress up pork with a rich honey and mustard sauce.

Marinating meat tenderises it and adds extra flavours, so if you can prepare your meat ahead and leave it in the marinade for a few hours before cooking, it will taste all the better.

Fruity Chicken Platter

Preparation time: 20 minutes. Freezing: not recommended. Serves 4.

This refreshing dish combines fragrant tropical fruits with creamy chicken and crisp salad ingredients. Serve with ciabatta bread.

1 small melon, peeled, de-seeded and cut into chunks

1 mango, peeled and sliced

¼ cucumber, cut into small chunks

½ red pepper, de-seeded and cut into small pieces

8 ready-to-eat dried apricots, cut into small pieces

375 g (12 oz) cooked chicken, cut into bite-size pieces

4 tablespoons sunflower oil

1 tablespoon white wine vinegar

3 tablespoons mayonnaise

½ teaspoon curry paste

1 tablespoon snipped fresh chives

a bag of rocket or ½ bag of mixed salad leaves

❶ Place the melon, mango, cucumber, red pepper and apricot pieces in a bowl.

❷ Place the chicken in a second bowl.

❸ Whisk together the oil and vinegar and stir 1 tablespoon into the mayonnaise, with the curry paste, until smooth.

❹ Add the mayonnaise mixture to the chicken and stir until evenly coated.

❺ Toss the melon mixture with the remaining oil-and-vinegar dressing and the chives.

❻ Arrange the rocket or salad leaves on a serving dish and spoon the melon mixture around the edge. Pile the mayonnaise-coated chicken in the centre.

Chicken in Red Pesto Sauce

Preparation and cooking time: 30 minutes.
Freezing: recommended, without the yogurt. Serves 4.

An easy way to dress up plain chicken breasts and turn them into something special. Accompany the chicken with potatoes and a green vegetable, or Bacon, Mushroom and Walnut Risotto (page 46).

2 tablespoons olive oil

4 boneless, skinless chicken breasts

200 ml (7 fl oz) hot chicken stock

3 tablespoons tomato purée

2 tablespoons red pesto

4 tablespoons greek-style yogurt

salt and pepper

2 tablespoons chopped fresh marjoram, to
garnish

❶ Heat the oil in a frying-pan and lightly brown the chicken breasts on both sides.
❷ Mix together the stock, tomato purée and red pesto and pour into the pan. Cover and simmer for 20 minutes or until the chicken is cooked.

❸ Lift the chicken breasts from the pan and place on a serving dish. Remove the pan from the heat and stir in the yogurt. Season and reheat gently without boiling.
❹ Spoon the sauce over the chicken and sprinkle with chopped marjoram to garnish.

Chicken with Rainbow Peppers

Preparation and cooking time: 25 minutes.
Freezing: recommended. Serves 4.

Chicken thighs cook quickly and are economical to buy, but use boned chicken breasts if you prefer. Serve with a packet of savoury rice, such as golden vegetable.

8 boneless chicken thighs

2 tablespoons seasoned plain flour

1 tablespoon vegetable oil

25 g (1 oz) butter

1 each red, yellow, green and orange peppers,
de-seeded and sliced thinly

1 leek, sliced thinly

400 g can of chopped tomatoes

1 tablespoon chopped fresh marjoram

❶ Toss the chicken thighs in the seasoned flour.
❷ Heat the oil and butter in a large frying-pan and fry the chicken until lightly browned.

❸ Add the peppers and leek to the pan with the tomatoes and marjoram, and bring to the boil.
❹ Lower the heat, cover the pan and simmer for about 15 minutes or until the chicken is cooked.

Balti Chicken

Preparation and cooking time: 30 minutes.
Freezing: recommended. Serves 4.

This chicken curry is quick to cook and has a mildly spiced, creamy flavour. If you don't have all the spices, use 2 tablespoons of mild curry powder or paste instead. Accompany this with hot garlic and coriander naan bread.

3 tablespoons vegetable oil

1 onion, chopped finely

1 teaspoon ground coriander

1 teaspoon ground cumin

1 teaspoon ground ginger

1 teaspoon turmeric

½ teaspoon chilli powder

1 garlic clove, crushed

1 courgette, sliced

230 g can of chopped tomatoes

1 teaspoon sugar

4 tablespoons water

500 g (1 lb) boneless, skinless chicken
    breasts, cut into small pieces

1 teaspoon cornflour

142 ml (5 fl oz) carton of soured cream

50 g (2 oz) creamed coconut, chopped

salt and pepper

❶ Heat 1 tablespoon of the oil in a large pan and fry the onion until soft. Stir in the spices and garlic and cook for 1 minute.

❷ Add the courgette, tomatoes, sugar and water. Bring to the boil and simmer for 10 minutes.

❸ While the curry sauce is cooking, heat the remaining oil in a wok or large frying-pan and stir-fry the chicken in batches until golden brown. Remove the chicken from the pan and add it to the curry sauce.

❹ Stir the cornflour into the soured cream and add it to the curry sauce, with the creamed coconut. Stir until the sauce is boiling and the creamed coconut has dissolved. Season to taste and serve at once.

Pork with Honey and Mustard Sauce

Preparation and cooking time: 25 minutes.
Freezing: recommended. Serves 4.

Pork tenderloin has virtually no waste, is very tender and cooks quickly. Pork steaks could also be used for the recipe – trim off any fat and cut the steaks through the centre into thin slices. Serve with new potatoes and a green vegetable.

625 g (1¼ lb) pork tenderloin

2 tablespoons oil

25 g (1 oz) butter

1 onion, sliced

250 g (8 oz) mushrooms, sliced or quartered

200 ml (7 fl oz) chicken or pork stock

150 ml (¼ pint) pineapple juice

2 tablespoons tomato purée

2 tablespoons soy sauce

2 tablespoons clear honey

2 teaspoons Dijon mustard

salt and pepper

❶ Trim any fat from the pork and slice the pork into 5 mm (¼-inch) slices. Place the slices between two sheets of clingfilm and beat them with a rolling pin until thin.

❷ Heat the oil in a large frying-pan and fry the pork over a medium heat until lightly browned on both sides. Remove the pork from the pan and keep it warm.

❸ Add the butter to the pan and fry the onion and mushrooms until softened. Add the stock, pineapple juice, tomato purée, soy sauce, honey, mustard and seasoning. Simmer for 1 minute.

❹ Return the pork to the pan and simmer gently for 2 to 3 minutes. Serve at once.

Sausage and Apple Burgers with Orange and Cranberry Sauce

Preparation and cooking time: 25 minutes.
Freezing: recommended (freeze burgers and sauce separately).
Serves 4.

These tasty sausage burgers can be served with mashed potatoes or oven chips.

500 g (1 lb) pork sausagemeat
1 small onion, chopped finely
1 tablespoon chopped fresh sage
1 dessert apple, peeled and chopped finely
1 tablespoon Dijon mustard
salt and pepper
oil for shallow-frying or grilling

For the sauce:
4 tablespoons cranberry sauce
grated zest and juice of ½ orange
a pinch of ground cinnamon

❶ In a bowl, mix together the sausagemeat, onion, sage, apple, mustard and seasoning until well combined.

❷ With floured hands, shape the mixture into 12 small burgers.

❸ Heat some oil in a frying-pan and shallow-fry the burgers for about 10 minutes, turning once. Alternatively, brush with oil and grill for the same time, turning once.

❹ While the sausage burgers are cooking, make the sauce. Heat the cranberry sauce, orange zest, orange juice and cinnamon in a small saucepan until the sauce has melted and the mixture is hot.

❺ Drain the burgers and serve with the cranberry sauce.

Sesame Stir-fried Lamb

Preparation and cooking time: 30 minutes.
Freezing: recommended (the uncooked lamb could be frozen in the marinade). Serves 4.

If you want to prepare part of this dish ahead, cut the lamb into strips and leave it marinating in the coriander and sauces so that it absorbs more of their flavour. This can be done several hours ahead or the night before. Serve this with boiled rice or noodles.

1 teaspoon ground coriander

3 tablespoons hoisin sauce

1 tablespoon dark soy sauce

750 g (1½ lb) lean lamb, cut into thin
   strips

3 tablespoons vegetable or groundnut oil

6 spring onions, cut into 2.5 cm (1-inch)
   lengths

1 red pepper, de-seeded and sliced

1 courgette, sliced

8 baby sweetcorn

125 g (4 oz) broccoli florets, blanched for 2
   minutes

2 tablespoons sesame seeds

❶ Stir the coriander into the hoisin and soy sauces. Add the lamb and stir until the meat is coated.

❷ Heat 2 tablespoons of the oil in a large frying-pan or wok and stir-fry the spring onions, red pepper, courgette and sweetcorn for 4 minutes or until starting to soften.

❸ Add the broccoli and stir-fry for a further 3 minutes.Transfer the vegetables from the pan to a plate and keep them warm.

❹ Add the remaining oil to the pan. Lift the lamb from its marinade and stir-fry over a brisk heat for 2 to 3 minutes. Sprinkle in the sesame seeds and toss the meat until coated with the seeds.

❺ Return the vegetables to the pan, plus any remaining marinade. Toss over the heat for 2 to 3 minutes and then serve at once.

Turkey Escalopes with Mushroom Sauce

Preparation and cooking time: 30 minutes.
Freezing: recommended, after step 4. Serves 4.

Turkey breast slices are cut thinly so that they cook quickly. In this recipe the turkey slices are sandwiched with ham and coated in a crisp breadcrumb and parmesan crust before being fried. Serve with your favourite vegetables.

For the sauce:

125 g (4 oz) baby button mushrooms
juice of 1 orange
150 ml (¼ pint) chicken stock
1 tablespoon coarse-grain mustard
142 ml (5 fl oz) carton of single cream
1 tablespoon cornflour
salt and pepper

For the escalopes:

2 tablespoons grated parmesan cheese
50 g (2 oz) dry breadcrumbs
8 turkey breast slices
2 slices of ham
2 tablespoons plain flour
1 egg, beaten
oil for shallow-frying

❶ To make the sauce, place the mushrooms in a saucepan with the orange juice and stock, and simmer for 10 minutes. Add the mustard. Mix the cream and the cornflour together until smooth and add it to the pan.

❷ Stir the sauce over a gentle heat until boiling. Simmer for 1 minute and season to taste.

❸ While the sauce is cooking, prepare the escalopes. Mix the parmesan and breadcrumbs together on a plate.

❹ Sandwich two turkey slices with half a slice of ham. Dust this with the flour, brush it with the beaten egg and press the crumb mixture over it until coated. Repeat with the remaining turkey and ham to make four 'sandwiches'.

❺ Heat some oil in a frying-pan and shallow-fry the escalopes for about 5 minutes, turning them over once. Drain the escalopes and place on serving plates. Spoon over the sauce and serve at once.

Pasta and Rice Dishes

Pasta is everyone's favourite – children and adults alike love it – and it's one of the quickest meals to prepare. Dried pasta takes about 10 minutes to cook, but the arrival of fresh pasta in the chiller cabinet has cut the cooking time even more.

Rice can be unexciting when plainly cooked, but mix it with chopped meat, nuts or vegetables and it makes a tasty risotto, an unusual stir-fry or an economical stuffing.

Tagliatelle with Tomato and Celery Sauce

Preparation and cooking time: 30 minutes.
Freezing: recommended, after step 4. Serves 4.

A colourful pasta dish that's easy to make and is full of rich, Mediterranean flavours. Serve each portion topped with shredded basil and shavings of fresh parmesan cheese.

2 tablespoons olive oil

2 celery sticks, chopped finely

1 carrot, chopped finely

1 onion, chopped finely

2 garlic cloves, crushed

2 tablespoons tomato purée

2 × 397 g can of chopped tomatoes with herbs

2 sun-dried tomatoes, sliced finely

500 g (1 lb) tagliatelle

12 black olives

salt and pepper

To garnish:

basil leaves

fresh parmesan cheese

❶ Heat the oil in a large frying-pan and fry the celery, carrot, onion and garlic for 2 to 3 minutes.

❷ Add the tomato purée, canned tomatoes, sun-dried tomatoes and seasoning. Bring to the boil, lower the heat and allow to bubble steadily for 25 minutes, or until the sauce has reduced and thickened, stirring occasionally.

❸ About 10 minutes before the sauce is ready, cook the pasta according to the instructions on the packet.

❹ Stir the olives into the tomato sauce and drain the tagliatelle. Add the pasta to the sauce and toss to mix.

❺ Serve at once, topped with basil leaves and shavings of parmesan cheese, shaved from a block of fresh parmesan using a vegetable peeler.

Bacon, Mushroom and Walnut Risotto

Preparation and cooking time: 30 minutes.
Freezing: not recommended. Serves 4.

This makes a good light supper on its own or with a salad. It could also be served as an accompaniment to dishes like Chicken in Red Pesto Sauce (page 32) or Pork with Honey and Mustard Sauce (page 36).

1 tablespoon olive oil

2 shallots or small onions, chopped finely

4 back bacon rashers, chopped

300 g (10 oz) mushrooms, sliced, e.g. button, open-cup, oyster, brown cap, or a mixture

2 garlic cloves, crushed

1 red pepper, de-seeded and chopped

175 g (6 oz) easy-cook long-grain and wild rice

600 ml (1 pint) chicken stock

2 tablespoons tomato purée

125 g (4 oz) sweetcorn

50 g (2 oz) walnut pieces

salt and pepper

❶ Heat the oil in a large frying-pan and cook the shallots or onions and bacon until lightly browned.

❷ Add the mushrooms, garlic and red pepper and cook for 3 minutes.

❸ Stir in the rice and then add the stock and tomato purée. Bring to the boil, lower the heat and simmer uncovered for 10 minutes.

❹ Add the sweetcorn, stir well and simmer for a further 10 minutes or until the rice is tender and the liquid has been absorbed.

❺ Season and sprinkle over the walnuts. Serve at once.

Cauliflower and Macaroni Gratin

Preparation and cooking time: 30 minutes.
Freezing: recommended. Serves 4.

This recipe could be made with broccoli instead of cauliflower, or a mixture of the two.

1 cauliflower, divided into small florets
125 g (4 oz) quick-cook macaroni
25 g (1 oz) butter
125 g (4 oz) mushrooms, sliced
295 g can of condensed cream of celery soup

185 g can of tuna chunks, drained
50 g (2 oz) red Leicester cheese, grated
2 tablespoons dry breadcrumbs
salt and pepper

❶ Cook the cauliflower florets in boiling water until just tender. Drain.
❷ While the cauliflower is cooking, cook the macaroni according to the packet instructions. Drain.
❸ Melt the butter in a large saucepan and fry the mushrooms until soft. Stir in the soup and bring to simmering point over a low heat.

❹ Stir in the cauliflower, macaroni, tuna and seasoning to taste. Preheat the grill to hot. Spoon the mixture into a shallow heatproof dish.
❺ Sprinkle with the cheese and breadcrumbs and brown lightly under the grill. Serve at once.

Chicken and Ham Carbonara

Preparation and cooking time: 15 minutes.
Freezing: recommended. Serves 4.

375 g (12 oz) penne (pasta quills)
2 tablespoons olive oil
2 boneless, skinless chicken breasts, cut into small pieces
50 g (2 oz) mange-tout peas, cut into 1 cm (½-inch) pieces

4 slices of Parma ham, cut into small pieces
200 ml (7 fl oz) carton of crème fraîche
1 teaspoon Dijon mustard
75 g (3 oz) Lancashire cheese, crumbled
salt and pepper
chopped fresh parsley, to garnish (optional)

❶ Cook the penne in lightly salted boiling water according to the packet instructions.
❷ While the pasta is cooking, heat the oil in a large frying-pan and stir-fry the chicken over a brisk heat for 4 to 5 minutes until lightly browned. Remove the chicken from the pan and keep it warm.
❸ Add the mange-tout peas and Parma ham to the pan and stir-fry for 1 minute.

Return the chicken to the pan, add the crème fraîche, mustard and seasoning to taste.
❹ Bring slowly to simmering point, stirring frequently, and allow to bubble gently until the pasta is ready. Drain the penne and stir into the pan with the cheese.
❺ Serve at once, sprinkled with chopped parsley if you like.

Fruity Rice Salad

Preparation time: 15 minutes. Freezing: not recommended. Serves 4.

Serve this light, refreshing rice dish with a plain green salad and chunks of french bread or crusty rolls.

277 g can of long-grain rice

227 g can of pineapple pieces in natural juice

250 g (8 oz) large peeled prawns

250 g (8 oz) cooked chicken, cut into strips

¼ cucumber, cut into thin strips

4 spring onions, sliced thinly

125 g (4 oz) button mushrooms, sliced thinly

2 tablespoons smooth peanut butter

1 tablespoon light soy sauce

1 tablespoon lemon juice

❶ Place the rice in a large bowl.
❷ Drain the pineapple, reserving 2 tablespoons of the juice.
❸ Mix the pineapple pieces, prawns, chicken, cucumber, spring onions and mushrooms into the rice.

❹ Mix the reserved pineapple juice with the peanut butter, soy sauce, lemon juice and 1 tablespoon of water until smooth. Pour over the salad and toss gently to mix.

Fusilli with Gammon and Sausage

Preparation and cooking time: 30 minutes. Freezing: recommended. Serves 4.

If you have any vegetables left over from a previous meal, these can be added to the dish instead of (or as well as) the peas.

250 g (8 oz) fusilli (pasta spirals)

4 large Lincolnshire sausages

1 tablespoon vegetable or sunflower oil

1 gammon steak or bacon chop, cut into small pieces

2 leeks, sliced thinly

125 g (4 oz) frozen peas

295 g can of condensed cream of mushroom soup

grated parmesan or Cheddar cheese, to serve

❶ Preheat the grill to hot. Meanwhile, cook the fusilli according to the instructions on the packet.
❷ While the pasta is cooking, grill the sausages and cut each one into four pieces.
❸ Heat the oil in a large saucepan or frying-pan and cook the gammon or

bacon and leeks until the meat is browned and the leeks are soft.
❹ Add the peas and soup to the pan and heat gently until simmering. Stir in the sausages, drained pasta and seasoning.
❺ Cook gently for 2 to 3 minutes. Serve at once, sprinkled with grated cheese.

Quick Seafood Paella

Preparation and cooking time: 30 minutes.
Freezing: not recommended. Serves 4.

Savoury rice adds flavour and colour to a dish, thus avoiding the
necessity of keeping a big stock of herbs and seasonings in your store
cupboard. In this recipe, saffron rice gives the dish an attractive golden
hue. Prepare the haddock and tomatoes while the rice is cooking, so
that they are ready to be added when the rice is almost done.

1 tablespoon vegetable or sunflower oil

25 g (1 oz) butter

1 onion, chopped

1 red pepper, de-seeded and chopped

1 courgette, cut into small chunks

125 g packet of saffron savoury rice

450 ml (¾ pint) fish or chicken stock

375 g (12 oz) haddock fillet, skinned and cut
   into large cubes

200 g (7 oz) pack of fresh seafood cocktail or
   small prawns

2 tablespoons chopped fresh dill

3 tomatoes, peeled and chopped

salt and pepper

❶ Heat the oil and butter in a large
frying-pan and cook the onion until soft.
❷ Stir in the red pepper, courgette and
rice.
❸ Pour in the stock, bring to the boil,
lower the heat and simmer gently for 15
minutes.

❹ Stir in the haddock, seafood cocktail
or prawns, dill, tomatoes and seasoning to
taste.
❺ Simmer for a further 5 minutes or
until the rice is tender and has absorbed
the stock. Serve at once.

Spaghetti with Seafood Sauce

Preparation and cooking time: 20 minutes.
Freezing: not recommended. Serves 4.

Use a packet of seafood cocktail (ready-prepared mixed seafood) or make up your own selection from prawns, squid, fish sticks and mussels.

397 g can of chopped tomatoes with herbs

75 ml (3 fl oz) passata (sieved tomatoes)

2 garlic cloves, crushed

50 g (2 oz) button mushrooms, halved or quartered

1 teaspoon sugar

500 g bag of fresh spaghetti

2 × 200 g (7 oz) pack of fresh seafood cocktail

salt and pepper

❶ Place the tomatoes, passata, garlic, mushrooms and sugar in a saucepan. Bring to simmering point, cover and cook gently for 10 minutes.

❷ When the tomato sauce is nearly ready, cook the spaghetti according to the packet instructions.

❸ Stir the seafood cocktail into the tomato sauce and add seasoning to taste.

❹ Drain the spaghetti and serve with the seafood sauce spooned over.

Spinach and Bolognese Gratin

Preparation and cooking time: 30 minutes.
Freezing: recommended. Serves 4.

An oven-baked version of spaghetti bolognese that's tasty and quick to make. Leave the spinach to defrost in a strainer, and then press with a wooden spoon or between two plates to extract as much water as possible.

250 g (8 oz) frozen spinach, defrosted and drained well

1 tablespoon oil

125 g (4 oz) mushrooms, sliced

2 × 300 g can of bolognese sauce

375 g (12 oz) bag of fresh spaghetti

600 ml (1 pint) cheese sauce

50 g (2 oz) Gruyère cheese, grated

❶ Preheat the oven to Gas Mark 6/200°C/400°F.

❷ Spoon the spinach over the base of a large, shallow ovenproof dish.

❸ Heat the oil in a pan and fry the mushrooms until soft. Add the bolognese sauce and bring slowly to the boil.

❹ While the sauce is heating, cook the spaghetti according to the packet instructions. Drain.

❺ Spoon the hot bolognese sauce over the spinach and top with the spaghetti. Pour over the cheese sauce and sprinkle with the grated Gruyère.

❻ Bake for 20 minutes or until it is golden brown and the cheese is bubbling.

Beefy Rice with Beans

Preparation and cooking time: 30 minutes.
Freezing: not recommended. Serves 4.

A filling, satisfying dish that the family will love. Minced lamb could be used instead of beef, if you prefer.

1 tablespoon oil
1 onion, sliced thinly
500 g (1 lb) lean minced beef
125 g (4 oz) button mushrooms, halved
3 tablespoons brown sauce
420 g can of beans in tomato sauce

150 ml (¼ pint) beef stock
2 tablespoons tomato purée
125 g bag of boil-in-the bag basmati rice
125 g (4 oz) frozen peas
salt and pepper

❶ Heat the oil in a large frying-pan and fry the onion until soft.

❷ Add the minced beef, breaking it up with a wooden spoon, and fry until lightly browned.

❸ Add the mushrooms, brown sauce, beans in tomato sauce, stock and tomato purée. Allow to simmer uncovered for 15 minutes, stirring occasionally.

❹ While the beef is cooking, cook the bag of rice in 1 litre (1¾ pints) of boiling water for 12 minutes. Lift the bag from the water and cut it open.

❺ Stir the rice into the beef mixture with the peas and seasoning to taste.

❻ Cook for a further 5 minutes until the peas are heated through. Serve at once.

Mainly Vegetables

Whether you follow a vegetarian diet or not, everyone can enjoy a main course or light snack that's based on beans, pulses or vegetables. In this section, some of the dishes are suitable for vegetarians, such as Chinese Vegetables with Crispy Noodles (below), Bean Burgers (page 60) and Creamy Vegetable Korma (page 62), and most of the others can be adapted to a vegetarian lifestyle by substituting tofu, nuts, beans or extra vegetables for the meat given in a recipe. For example, in Spinach, Bacon and Blue Cheese Salad with Croûtons (page 70), use a mixture of walnuts, chopped celery and cubes of vegetarian Cheddar cheese in place of the bacon.

Chinese Vegetables with Crispy Noodles

Preparation and cooking time: 30 minutes.
Freezing: not recommended. Serves 4.

Use fresh spaghetti from the chiller cabinet for this recipe. Dried fine egg-noodles could also be used, but they will need to be cooked first, according to the packet instructions. Make sure that they are thoroughly dry before you fry them or they will spit in the hot oil.

oil for deep-frying
250 g (8 oz) fresh spaghetti
2 tablespoons sesame or sunflower oil
750 g (1½ lb) mixed vegetables, e.g.
   mange-tout peas, mushrooms, baby
   sweetcorn, spring onions, broccoli and
   peppers, cut into small pieces

1 tablespoon lemon juice
2 tablespoons light soy sauce
2 tablespoons oyster sauce

❶ Heat the oil for deep-frying in a large saucepan or deep-fat fryer to 190°C/375°F – it is important that the oil is heated to the correct temperature or the cooked noodles will be tough and chewy rather than crisp. If you don't have a thermometer, heat until a small cube of bread browns in the oil in 30 seconds.

❷ Break the noodles into short lengths and deep-fry in several batches for 2 to 3 minutes, until golden brown and crisp. Drain them on kitchen paper and keep them warm in a low oven (don't cover them or they will go soggy).

❸ Heat the sesame or sunflower oil in a wok or large frying-pan and stir-fry the vegetables for 5 to 8 minutes until they start to soften.

❹ Mix together the lemon juice, soy sauce and oyster sauce and pour over the vegetables.

❺ Stir-fry for 1 minute until the vegetables are coated with the sauces. Pile on top of the noodles and serve at once.

Bean Burgers

Preparation and cooking time: 30 minutes.
Freezing: recommended. Serves 4.

An easy way to shape the burgers is to press the mixture into an 8 cm (3-inch) pastry cutter. Serve with oven chips, salad and relishes.

432 g can of chick-peas, drained and rinsed

432 g can of red kidney beans, drained and rinsed

1 courgette, grated

50 g (2 oz) chopped mixed nuts

2 teaspoons tomato purée

1 tablespoon chopped fresh coriander

4 spring onions, chopped finely

1 egg, beaten

40 g (1½ oz) medium oatmeal

oil for shallow-frying

salt and pepper

❶ In a food processor, chop the chick-peas finely. Mash the kidney beans in a bowl and add the chopped chick-peas, grated courgette, nuts, tomato purée, coriander, spring onions, seasoning and beaten egg to bind. Stir until evenly combined.

❷ With floured hands, divide the mixture into 8 and shape them into burgers. Press the oatmeal over the burgers to coat them.

❸ Heat the oil in a frying-pan and shallow-fry the burgers for 8 to 10 minutes until golden brown, turning once. Alternatively, brush with oil and grill for the same time.

Tuscan Bean Soup

Preparation and cooking time: 30 minutes.
Freezing: recommended. Serves 4.

A filling, main-meal soup that needs no accompaniment, apart from lots of crusty wholegrain bread.

2 tablespoons olive oil

2 celery sticks, chopped

1 red onion, sliced thinly

2 carrots, chopped

2 courgettes, chopped

432 g can of cannellini beans, drained and rinsed

250 g (8 oz) smoked pork sausage, cut into 2.5 cm (1-inch) lengths

2 × 450 g carton of fresh tomato soup with basil

salt and pepper

parmesan cheese, grated, to serve (optional)

❶ Heat the oil in a large saucepan and fry the celery, onion and carrots for 5 minutes until they start to soften.

❷ Add the courgettes, cover the pan and cook gently for a further 5 minutes.

❸ Add the beans, sausage and soup and bring slowly to simmering point. Cook for a further 10 minutes. Season to taste.

❹ Ladle the soup into deep soup bowls and sprinkle with parmesan cheese if you like.

Creamy Vegetable Korma

Preparation and cooking time: 30 minutes.
Freezing: recommended. Serves 4.

Par-boiling the vegetables first cuts down the cooking time for this mild creamy curry. Serve with boiled rice, mango chutney and naan bread.

250 g (8 oz) carrots, sliced
250 g (8 oz) potatoes, cut into chunks
175 g (6 oz) cauliflower, cut into florets
2 tablespoons vegetable or sunflower oil
1 onion, chopped
2 tablespoons mild curry powder or paste
1 tablespoon lemon juice

50 g (2 oz) ground almonds
125 g (4 oz) frozen peas
432 g can of butter beans, drained and rinsed
300 ml (½ pint) tomato juice
200 ml (7 fl oz) double cream
salt and pepper
chopped fresh coriander, to garnish

❶ Cook the carrots, potatoes and cauliflower in lightly salted boiling water until just tender.

❷ While the vegetables are cooking, heat the oil in a large pan and fry the onion until soft.

❸ Stir in the curry powder or paste and cook for 1 minute. Add the lemon juice, ground almonds, peas, butter beans and tomato juice.

❹ Stir in the vegetables and bring to the boil over a gentle heat. Slowly stir in the cream and the seasoning.

❺ Simmer gently for 5 minutes. Serve sprinkled with chopped fresh coriander.

Crunchy Vegetable Fritters with Raita

Preparation and cooking time: 30 minutes.
Freezing: not recommended. Serves 6.

Serve these vegetable fritters on their own for a light meal, or as an accompaniment to plainly grilled pork or lamb chops.

For the batter:
125 g (4 oz) plain flour
1 tablespoon vegetable oil
200 ml (7 fl oz) water
1 egg white
oil for deep-frying
For the vegetables:
125 g (4 oz) aubergine, cut into 1 cm
   (½-inch) chunks

125 g (4 oz) button mushrooms
125 g (4 oz) cauliflower, cut into small florets
1 courgette, cut into 1 cm (½-inch) slices
For the sauce:
150 g (5 oz) carton of natural yogurt
1 tablespoon chopped fresh mint

❶ To make the batter, put the flour in a bowl and make a well in the centre. Add the oil and stir in with the water, a little at a time, to make a thick batter.

❷ Whisk the egg white until it stands in soft peaks and then fold it into the batter.

❸ Heat the oil for deep-frying in a large saucepan or deep-fat fryer to 190°C/375°F or until a small cube of bread browns in the oil in 45 seconds.

❹ Dip the vegetables into the batter and fry for 2 to 3 minutes until golden brown. Drain them on kitchen paper. Keep the fritters warm in a low oven, in an uncovered dish, as they cook.

❺ To make the sauce, spoon the yogurt into a small bowl and stir in the chopped mint. Season to taste and serve with the vegetable fritters.

Feta, Tomato and Aubergine Pizza

Preparation and cooking time: 30 minutes.
Freezing: not recommended. Serves 2.

Tangy feta cheese makes a slightly more unusual topping for pizzas than the traditional mozzarella. These two pizzas will serve four people if served with a salad.

2 ready-made pizza bases, about 23 cm
(9-inches) in diameter
3 tablespoons olive oil
2 teaspoons pesto
1 large garlic clove, chopped finely
400 g can of plum tomatoes, drained

1 small aubergine, sliced thinly
1 red onion, sliced thinly
125 g (4 oz) feta cheese, crumbled
1 tablespoon chopped fresh oregano
pepper

❶ Preheat the oven to Gas Mark 7/220°C/425°F. Place the pizza bases on lightly greased baking sheets.
❷ Mix 1 tablespoon of the olive oil with the pesto and garlic and brush the mixture over the pizza bases.
❸ Slice the tomatoes and arrange them over the bases, with the aubergine and onion slices. Divide the feta cheese between the pizzas and scatter over the oregano. Season with pepper.
❹ Brush the remaining oil over the aubergine and onion slices and bake in the oven for 15 to 20 minutes.

Flaky Tomato Tart

Preparation and cooking time: 30 minutes.
Freezing: recommended (reheat from frozen). Serves 4.

A quick and easy tart that has a deliciously flaky crust and needs no special tin, just a baking sheet. Serve with coleslaw or potato salad.

250 g (8 oz) chilled puff pastry

1 egg, beaten, to glaze

1 tablespoon olive oil

4 spring onions, sliced thinly

2 tablespoons red pesto

1 tablespoon tomato purée

3 tomatoes, sliced

1 courgette, sliced thinly

50 g (2 oz) mushrooms, sliced thinly

50 g (2 oz) grated pizza cheese

❶ Preheat the oven to Gas Mark 7/220°C/425°F.

❷ Roll out the pastry to a 23 cm (9-inch) round and lift it on to a baking sheet. Prick the pastry all over with a fork and brush the top with beaten egg – don't brush the pastry sides or it will not rise evenly.

❸ Bake for about 10 minutes, until risen and golden.

❹ While the pastry is cooking, mix together the oil, spring onions, pesto and tomato purée.

❺ Spoon the pesto mixture over the baked pastry round, spreading it to within 2 cm (¾ inch) of the edge.

❻ Top with the tomato, courgette and mushroom slices and sprinkle with the cheese.

❼ Return to the oven for about 10 minutes or until the tomatoes and courgettes have softened and the cheese has melted. Serve hot.

Spinach, Bacon and Blue Cheese Salad with Croûtons

Preparation and cooking time: 30 minutes.
Freezing: not recommended. Serves 4.

For vegetarians, omit the bacon from the salad. Add 125 g (4 oz) sliced mushrooms and a chopped pepper and fry them in the oil. Add extra cheese at the end.

4 tablespoons olive oil

1 garlic clove, crushed

4 slices of bread, crusts removed, cut into
    small cubes

250 g (8 oz) smoked bacon, chopped

4 tablespoons red wine vinegar

125 ml (4 fl oz) sunflower oil

2 teaspoons light soy sauce

1 teaspoon light brown sugar

175 g (6 oz) baby spinach leaves, shredded

125 g (4 oz) Danish blue cheese, crumbled

❶ Heat the olive oil in a small frying-pan. Add the garlic and bread cubes and fry until the bread is crisp and golden. Drain the croûtons on kitchen paper.

❷ Drain most of the oil from the pan, add the bacon and fry until crisp. Drain.

❸ Whisk together the vinegar, sunflower oil, soy sauce and sugar.

❹ Divide the spinach between four serving plates and scatter over the croûtons, bacon and cheese. Spoon over the dressing and serve at once.

Watercress and Orange Soup

Preparation and cooking time: 30 minutes.
Freezing: recommended. Serves 4.

A hearty vegetable soup, with the tangy taste of watercress and orange. Serve it with focaccia bread, brushed with olive oil, sprinkled with crushed garlic and chopped fresh thyme and warmed in a moderate oven for 10 minutes.

600 ml (1 pint) chicken or vegetable stock
2 large potatoes, peeled and chopped
a bunch of watercress, coarse stalks removed
150 ml (¼ pint) orange juice
25 g (1 oz) butter

2 leeks, sliced thinly
1 courgette, cut into small chunks
125 g (4 oz) sweetcorn
142 ml (5 fl oz) carton of double cream
salt and pepper

❶ Bring the stock to the boil in a large saucepan, add the potatoes and simmer until tender.

❷ Chop the watercress and add it to the pan. Simmer for 3 minutes.

❸ Pour the soup into a food processor, add the orange juice and purée until smooth.

❹ Rinse out the saucepan and return to a low heat. Add the butter and, when foaming, fry the leeks and courgette until soft.

❺ Pour the puréed soup into the saucepan and add the sweetcorn, cream and seasoning to taste.

❻ Reheat without boiling and serve at once.

Ten-Minute Puddings
A selection of almost instant desserts that will liven up a simple midweek supper with almost no effort.

Crushed Berry Meringues

Preparation time: 10 minutes. Freezing: not recommended. Serves 4.

284 ml (10 fl oz) carton of double cream
142 ml (5 fl oz) carton of fresh soured cream
a few drops of almond essence

250 g (8 oz) mixed berries
4 meringue shells, crushed

❶ Whip the double cream with the soured cream and a few drops of almond essence until stiff.

❷ Fold in most of the mixed berries and the crushed meringue shells. Spoon the mixture into sundae dishes and top with the remaining berries.

Mini-Alaskas

Preparation and cooking time: 10 minutes. Freezing: not recommended. Serves 4.

4 thick slices of jam-filled swiss roll
1 banana, sliced
4 scoops of ice cream (not soft-scoop)

2 egg whites
125 g (4 oz) caster sugar

❶ Preheat the oven to Gas Mark 6/200°C/400°F. Place each slice of swiss roll on a heatproof serving plate. Arrange the banana on top of the swiss roll slices, and spoon the ice cream over the top of the banana slices. Place the plates in the freezer for a few minutes while you prepare the meringue.

❷ Whisk the egg whites until stiff. Gradually whisk the caster sugar into the egg whites until the mixture stands in glossy peaks.

❸ Remove the plates from the freezer and pile the meringue over the ice cream to cover completely, bringing it down over the swiss roll slices to make a tight seal. Place the plates in the oven for about 4 minutes or until the meringue is lightly browned.

Red and Green Fruit Salad

**Preparation time: 10 minutes. Freezing: not recommended.
Serves 4.**

8 tablespoons seedless raspberry jam
grated zest and juice of 1 orange
6 tablespoons orange or apple juice

a mixture of red and green fruits, e.g.
   strawberries, raspberries, seedless grapes,
   melon chunks, kiwi fruit slices and plum
   slices

❶ Mix the raspberry jam with the orange zest and juice and the 6 tablespoons of orange or apple juice.

❷ Combine the sauce with the fruit, and spoon it into serving bowls.

Nectarine Brûlée

**Preparation and cooking time: 10 minutes.
Freezing: not recommended. Serves 4.**

4 large or 6 small nectarines, pitted and sliced
142 ml (5 fl oz) carton of double cream

150 g (5 oz) carton of peach or mango yogurt
3 tablespoons demerara sugar

❶ Preheat the grill. Place the nectarine slices in a shallow flameproof dish.
❷ Lightly whip the double cream until just thickened. Stir in the peach or mango yogurt. Pour the mixture over the nectarines and sprinkle with demerara sugar.

❸ Grill for 4 to 5 minutes, or until the sugar melts and begins to caramelise.

Pineapple Doughnut Rings

**Preparation time: 10 minutes. Freezing: not recommended.
Serves 4.**

4 ring doughnuts

432 g can of pineapple slices in natural juice

3 tablespoons sweet sherry

142 ml (5 fl oz) carton of double cream

❶ Cut the doughnuts in half through the centre. Drain the juice from the can of pineapple slices and mix it with the sweet sherry. Soak the doughnuts in the juice for 5 minutes.

❷ Reserve 4 pineapple slices and chop the rest. Whip the double cream until stiff, then fold in the chopped pineapple.

❸ Use the cream mixture to sandwich the doughnut halves, reserving some to spoon into the holes. Top with the reserved pineapple slices, replace the top halves of the doughnuts and fill the holes with the reserved cream and pineapple mixture.

Strawberry and Lemon Soufflé Omelette

**Preparation and cooking time: 10 minutes.
Freezing: not recommended. Serves 4.**

4 eggs, separated

1 teaspoon grated lemon zest

3 tablespoons caster sugar

25 g (1 oz) butter

3 tablespoons strawberry jam

75 g (3 oz) strawberries, sliced

icing sugar, to decorate

❶ Whisk the egg yolks with the lemon zest and caster sugar until pale and thick. Whisk the egg whites until stiff and fold them gently into the yolk mixture. Preheat the grill.

❷ Heat the butter in a large heavy frying-pan and, when foaming, pour in the egg mixture. Cook for a few seconds until the edges start to puff up. Slide the pan under the grill and cook until just set.

❸ Mix the strawberry jam with the sliced strawberries and spread this over one half of the omelette. Fold the omelette over and slide it on to a serving dish. Dredge with icing sugar and serve at once.

Index